The
Color Piaı

MW01283554

PlayBook ²

Bass Clef - Left Hand

2nd Edition

A Piano-In-Color Product

Julia Tulloch

ISBN: 1530919258

ISBN-13: 978-1530919253

DEDICATION

To Jesus, for everything.

To Jamie - Asher.
You are joy to my heart.

.

Dear Parents, Teachers and Students,

This second book of the **Color Piano Playbook Series** presents the bass clef and music for the left hand. This book builds on the skills introduced in Playbook 1 and makes reference to the topics introduced there, so be sure to complete Playbook 1 before beginning this one. While working through this book, it is a good idea to continue to practice the pieces in Playbook 1 in order to maintain the skills learned there.

This 2nd Edition has been re-ordered and simplified to make it even easier for children to learn, and lots of free supplementary material (games, worksheets and music) is available from www.PianoInColor.com/extras.

The www.pianoInColor.com/playBook site contains recordings of all the music in this book, so the student can enjoy listening to them and playing along with the play-along tracks.

Get your pencil, dice, counters and piano, and let the fun continue!

Julia Tulloch

www.pianoInColor.com/playBook

Contents

Setting Up

In PlayBook 1, you slotted a Colored Key Strip behind the Treble Clef notes beginning at Middle C. Now we will set up a Colored Key Strip for the Bass Clef notes.

Cut out the Colored Key Strip on page 35 and fold it on the dotted lines with the letters facing you. Find the group of 2 black keys to the left of Middle C. Keeping the letters facing you, slot the Colored Key Strip behind those keys, matching the strip with the letters in the diagram below.

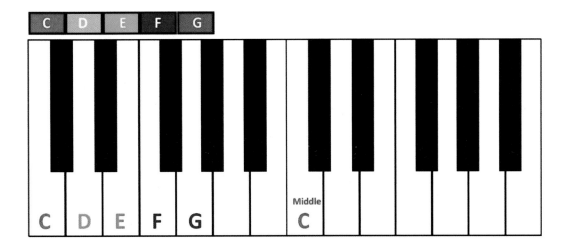

Now you are ready to begin learning the Bass Clef notes!

Finger Numbers

Each finger has a special number:

- Finger 1 - Thumb

- Finger 2 - Pointer Finger

- Finger 3 - Middle Finger

- Finger 4 - Ring Finger

- Finger 5 - Little Finger

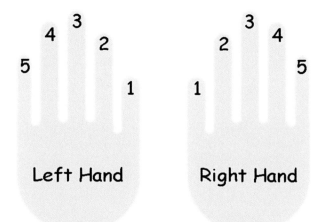

Trace your **left hand** in the box on the next page, and write the correct finger number on each finger. Then practice your left hand finger numbers by playing the FingerPrints board game in PlayBook 1 and using your left hand fingers to move the counters.

(You can also print the FingerPrints board game from www.PianoInColor.com/extras).

Music Theory Quiz

How much can you remember from PlayBook 1? Look at the keyboard below. Some of the note names are missing. Write in the missing names.

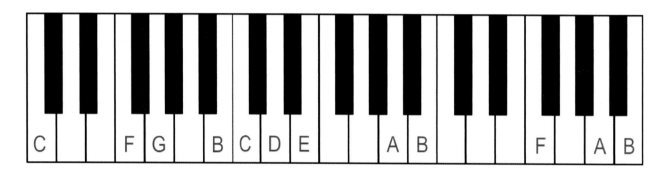

| C | | | F | G | | B | C | D | E | | | A | B | | | | F | | A | B |

Look at the Space Notes below. Write in the number of the space each note is sitting in.

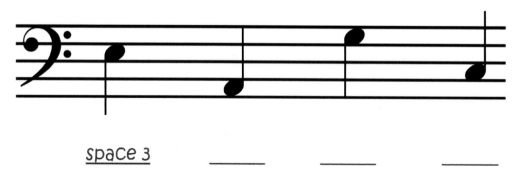

space 3   _____   _____   _____

Circle the staves containing next-door notes.

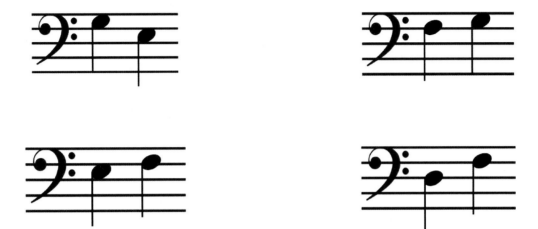

Look at the Line Notes below. Write in the number of the line each note is sitting on.

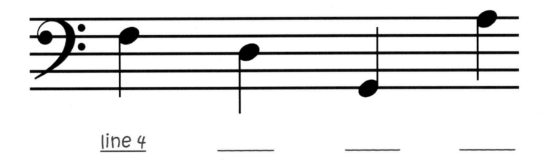

line 4   _____   _____   _____

Left Hand Notes

You are going to learn 5 Bass Clef notes: C, D, E, F and G. Here they are on the staff:

As the notes move up the staff, they follow a pattern: space note, line note, space note, line note, space note.

Here are those 5 notes on the keyboard:

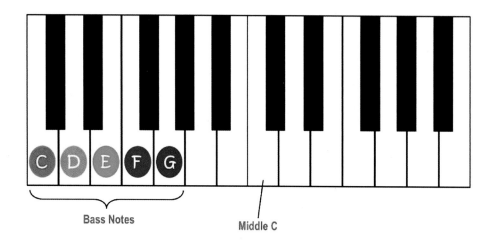

C and D

Here are C and D on the keyboard:

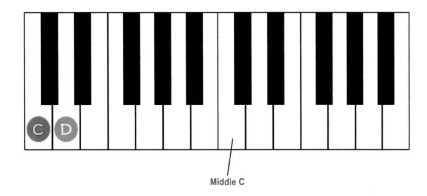

Middle C

This C sits in the 2nd space of the Bass Clef staff. It looks different from the other Bass Clef notes because the stem points upwards.

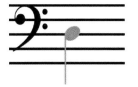

This D sits on line 3 of the Bass Clef staff.

Its stem points downwards like most of the Bass Clef notes we will learn in this book.

C & D Worksheet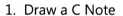

1. Draw a C Note

2. Draw a D Note

3. Use red to color the circles with C's inside. Use orange to color the circles with D's inside.

Listen to the recordings of **C Song** and **D Song** before you try to play them. Place finger 3 on C and finger 2 on D. Keep your fingers slightly curved and close to the keys as you play with your fingertips.

C Song

D Song

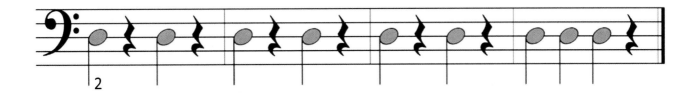

Listen to the recording of **Duet** before you play it. Balancing a small eraser on the back of your hand as you play it, will remind you to keep a good hand position with curved fingers.

Duet

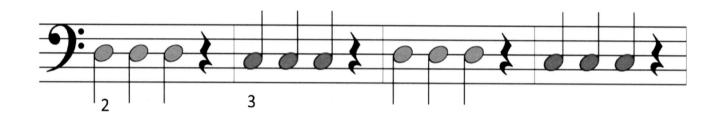

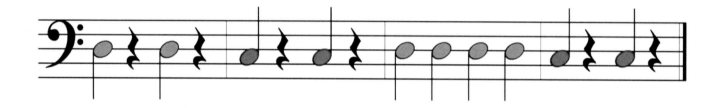

You can use other fingers to play **Duet**.

Try starting with finger 3 on the D, and playing it with next-door fingers 3 and 4.

C & D Checklist

I can play these songs with the

play-along tracks:

☐ **C Song**

☐ **D Song**

☐ **Duet**

When **all** the boxes are checked, move on to the next page.

E

Here is E on the keyboard:

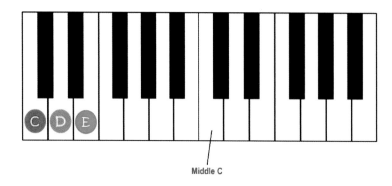

Middle C

This E sits in the 3rd space of the Bass Clef staff.

Draw an E note on this staff

Practice **The Slide** until you can play it without looking down at your hands.

The Slide

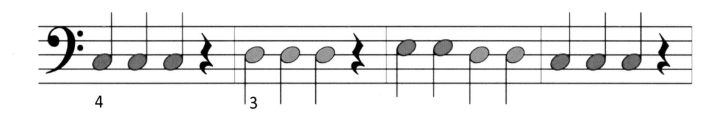

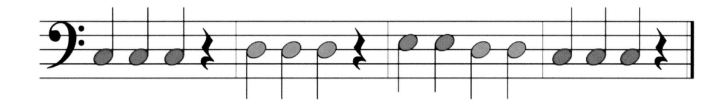

You can use other fingers to play **The Slide**.

Try starting with finger 3 on C, and using next-door fingers 3, 2 and 1.

Listen to the recording of **Itsy Bitsy Spider**, following the music notes on the page with your finger. Can you sing along while you play?

Imagine your hand is a spider tip-toeing across the keys, and be sure to stay on your fingertips!

Itsy Bitsy Spider

Out   came the sun - shine and dried up all the   rain

It - sy Bit - sy Spi - der climbed up the spout a - gain

C D E Worksheet

Can you recognize the Bass Clef notes when they are not in rainbow-colors? Link the balloons to their strings.

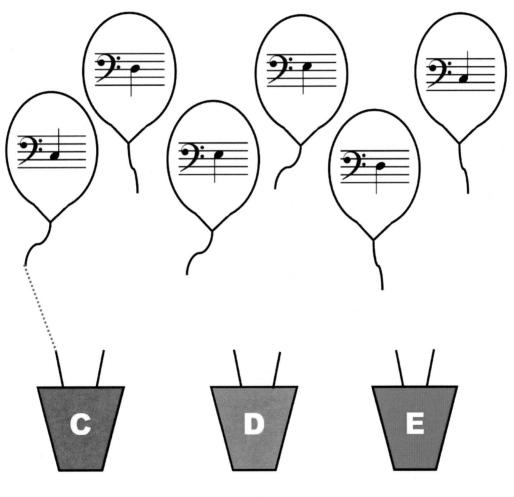

You learned **Follow Me** in PlayBook 1. Here it is again, but this time, for Left Hand. C and D are no longer in rainbow-colors. Can you still recognize them?

Follow Me

E Checklist

☐ I can play **The Slide** without looking at my hands

☐ I can play **Itsy Bitsy Spider** and sing along while I play

☐ I recognize the black notes in **Follow Me** and I am playing on my fingertips

When **all** the boxes are checked, move on to the next page.

F and G

Here are F and G on the keyboard:

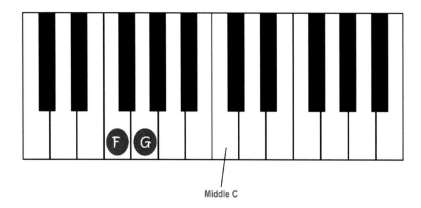

Middle C

F sits on line 4 of the Bass Clef staff. F is easy to recognize because it's circle is on the same line as the circle on the bass clef symbol.

G sits in the 4th space of the Bass Clef staff.

F & G Worksheet

1. Draw an F Note

2. Draw a G Note

3. Color the F arches blue. Color the G arches purple.

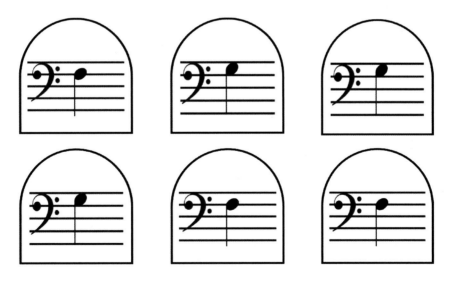

The Purple Blues begins with finger 1 on G. Remember to use the side of the tip of your thumb to play G.

The Purple Blues

1

Upside Down is another piece from PlayBook 1. Did you notice the Repeat Sign at the end of the second line? Can you remember what it means?

Upside Down

Blast Off uses all five Bass Clef notes. Don't miss the Repeat Sign at the end of the second line.

Blast Off

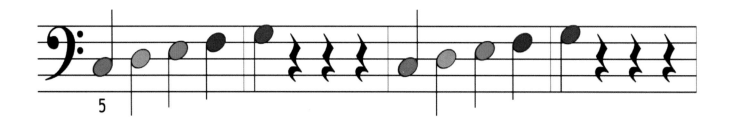

F & G Checklist

☐ I can play **The Purple Blues** with the play-along track

☐ I recognize the black notes in **Upside Down** and **Blast Off**

☐ I can play **Blast Off** without looking at my hands

When **all** the boxes are checked, move on to the next page.

Bass Clef Flash Cards Challenge

Cut out the Bass Clef flash cards on page 37. Your teacher will test you on recognizing the note names. Can you name them all correctly in less than a minute?

SWAP!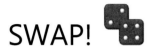

Play Swap! to practice the Bass Clef note names. You will need counters and a dice.

1. Place a counter for each player on the "START" square.

2. Each player takes a turn to throw the dice and move their counter forwards.

   - If you land on a note, you must name the note correctly to stay there. If you name it incorrectly, go back to where you were at the start of your turn.

   - If you land on a Rest Symbol, you must skip your next turn .

   - If you land on a SWAP! square, you can swap counter positions with any other player in the game.

3 The first one to arrive at the "END" is the winner.

30

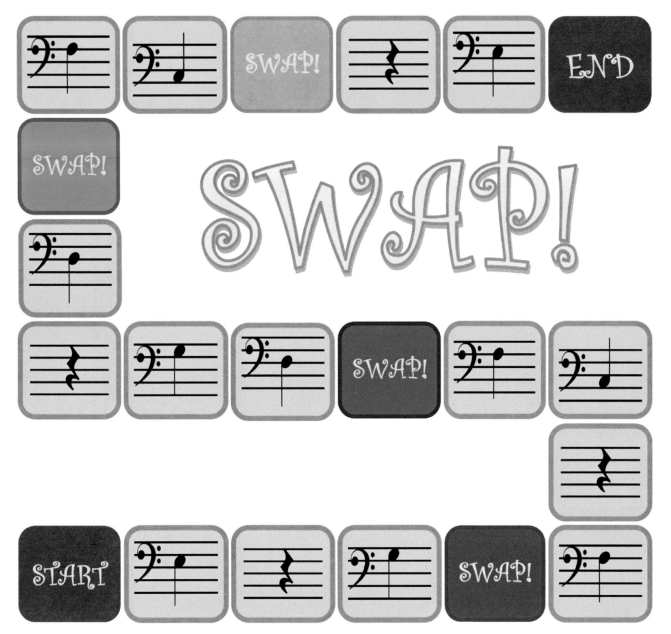

Before playing **Jingle Bells**, listen to the recording, following the music notes on the page with your finger. There are no rainbow-colors on the second line, so read the notes very carefully.

Jingle Bells

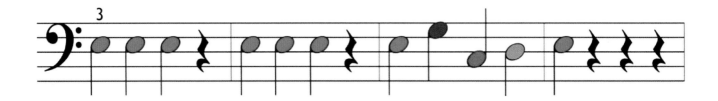

It's time to create your own music. The song below has words, but no music. Using the 5 notes you have learned, compose some music for it. Draw one note above each syllable. When you have finished drawing the notes, let your teacher sing along while you play it.

Practice, Practice

I   prac-   tice   and   prac-   tice   so

I   can   play   the   pi-   an-   o.

Checklist

☐ I can recognize all the notes on the

Bass Clef Flash Cards

☐ I can play **Jingle Bells** with the

play-along track

☐ I composed and played my own song

CONGRATULATIONS.

YOU DID IT!

Cut Outs

If you don't want to cut from the book, visit **www.pianoincolor.com/extras** to print Colored Key Strips and Flash Cards. While on the site, you can find more playBook games, worksheets, music and activities to help you on your musical journey.

Colored Key Strip

Cut out the Colored Key Strip below and fold it on the dotted line. Position it as directed on page 7.

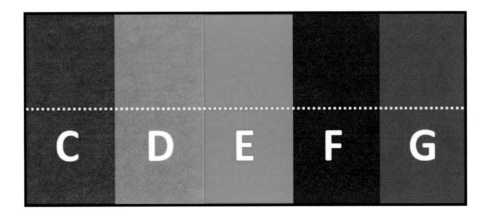

This page is intentionally left blank.

Bass Clef Flash Cards

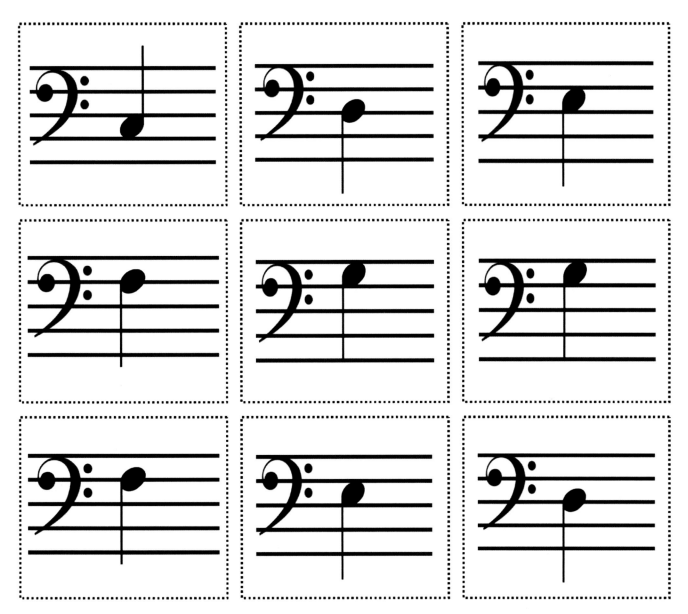

This page is intentionally left blank.

Made in United States
Orlando, FL
24 January 2023

29007476R00022